CW00383130

A LITTLE BOOK
OF LITANIES

Edited by
Amette Ley

*All booklets are published thanks to the
generous support of the members of the
Catholic Truth Society*

CATHOLIC TRUTH SOCIETY
PUBLISHERS TO THE HOLY SEE

Contents

All rights reserved. First published 2016 by The Incorporated Catholic Truth Society, 40-46 Harleyford Road London SE11 5AY Tel: 020 7640 0042 Fax: 020 7640 0046. © 2016 The Incorporated Catholic Truth Society.

ISBN 978 1 78469 112 7

LITANIES - A SHORT HISTORY

How litanies developed

A litany is simply a prayer. The word derives from the Greek *lite* which means "supplication". This gave rise to the word *litaneia*, "prayer, entreaty"; and this word, in turn, made its way via its late Latin form, *litania*, into our own language. Specifically, it now refers to a certain form of prayer as repetitive dialogue, which has its roots both in the natural inclination of humanity to find many and various ways of praising and making supplication to its deities, and also more particularly in the human response of gratitude to the supernatural revelation God gives of himself to his people.

Psalms

We find early examples of prayer in the form of a litany in the Old Testament; for instance Psalm 136, which praises God for the many works he has done.[1]

Psalm 136

O give thanks to the Lord, for he is good,
for his steadfast love endures for ever.
O give thanks to the God of gods,
for his steadfast love endures for ever.
O give thanks to the Lord of lords,
for his steadfast love endures for ever;
to him who alone does great wonders,
for his steadfast love endures for ever;
to him who by understanding made the heavens,
for his steadfast love endures for ever;
to him who spread out the earth upon the waters,
for his steadfast love endures for ever;
to him who made the great lights,
for his steadfast love endures for ever;
the sun to rule over the day,
for his steadfast love endures for ever;
the moon and stars to rule over the night,
for his steadfast love endures for ever;
to him who smote the first-born of Egypt,
for his steadfast love endures for ever;
and brought Israel out from among them,

for his steadfast love endures for ever;
with a strong hand and an outstretched arm,
for his steadfast love endures for ever;
to him who divided the Red Sea in sunder,
for his steadfast love endures for ever;
and made Israel pass through the midst of it,
for his steadfast love endures for ever;
but overthrew Pharaoh and his host in the Red Sea,
for his steadfast love endures for ever;
to him who led his people through the wilderness,
for his steadfast love endures for ever;
to him who smote great kings,
for his steadfast love endures for ever;
and slew famous kings,
for his steadfast love endures for ever;
Sihon, king of the Amorites,
for his steadfast love endures for ever;
and Og, king of Bashan,
for his steadfast love endures for ever;
and gave their land as a heritage,
for his steadfast love endures for ever;
a heritage to Israel his servant,
for his steadfast love endures for ever.
It is he who remembered us in our low estate,
for his steadfast love endures for ever;
and rescued us from our foes,
for his steadfast love endures for ever;

he who gives food to all flesh,
for his steadfast love endures for ever.
O give thanks to the God of heaven,
for his steadfast love endures for ever.

It would seem that this psalm could have been intended for public recitation with someone listing the works of God and all responding after each one.

Canticles

Another example is the song or "canticle" of those thrown into a furnace by King Nebuchadnezzar, recounted in the book of Daniel;[2] as the flames burned around them, they chose to sing the praises of God:

O all you works of the Lord, O bless the Lord
To him be highest glory and praise forever.

And you, angels of the Lord, O bless the Lord…
And you, the heavens of the Lord, O bless the Lord…
And you clouds of the sky, O bless the Lord…
And you, all armies of the Lord, O bless the Lord…
And you, sun and moon, O bless the Lord…
And you, the stars of the heav'ns, O bless the Lord…
And you, showers and rain, O bless the Lord…
And you, all you breezes and winds, O bless the Lord…
And you, fire and heat, O bless the Lord…
And you, cold and heat, O bless the Lord…

And you, showers and dew, O bless the Lord…
And you, frosts and cold, O bless the Lord…
And you, frost and snow, O bless the Lord…
And you, night-time and day, O bless the Lord…
And you, darkness and light, O bless the Lord…
And you, lightning and clouds, O bless the Lord…

Both these passages, although not usually referred to as litanies, nevertheless demonstrate the origins of the litany, and its repetitive, meditative and spiritually enriching character. Both of them are regularly used in the Liturgy of the Hours (the Divine Office), the official prayer of the Church.

Eastern Churches

The Eastern Churches retain this tradition even within their Divine Liturgy. At the end of the first part, what we would call the Liturgy of the Word, various petitions are made and the response to these, "*Kyrie eleison*", is given by the people. In fact, the litany-form of repetitive prayer and response occurs throughout the Eastern liturgy.[3] Within the Roman Catholic Church the threefold *Kyrie eleison, Christe eleison, Kyrie eleison* is a relic of what was probably a longer litany. The formula of the prayers for the needs of all people on Good Friday derives from a litany, and a litany is retained for baptisms within the Easter Vigil Mass.

Processions

Litanies were closely connected with processions in the early Church. The custom developed in Rome, especially after persecution ended, of processing to a different Church each day, particularly during Lent, carrying pictures and other aids to worship, and praying at the church, or "station" ("stopping-point"). The practice and wording of litanies thus became well known, and many different forms developed throughout the Christian world, honouring various aspects of God and paying tribute to many different saints, some local and some more widely known.

Then as now, the wording of some of these litanies sometimes departed from orthodox belief. By the early seventeenth century there were at least eighty litanies being used and there was a danger of abuse. In 1601, Pope Clement VIII decreed that publication was to be permitted for only two: the Litany of the Saints and the Litany to Our Lady known as the Litany of Loreto.

Shape of the Litany

Litanies are intended as a spiritual, meditative form of prayer, one in which those taking part can become ever more focused on the love and mercy of God. Usually a litany is formed of a list of invocations and petitions, either addressed to God, or to a particular saint or saints. The litany is usually led by one person, either a priest or a lay person, and the rest of the company make the responses; however, there is no reason why litanies cannot be used by individuals praying alone. As with the Rosary, the prayers should never be rushed and so the attention of the mind, if wandering, can be brought gently back by the rhythm of the words.

The prayers of the litany may focus on certain seasons, or on specific needs in which the saints may help us, or they may simply be intended for the praise of God. A litany typically begins with the sign of the cross, followed by invocations for mercy to the three Persons of the Trinity. Then follow the particular prayers. The responses vary according to whether God or one of his creatures is being addressed at that moment. When God is addressed, the response may be "have mercy on us", "save us", "graciously hear us" or "spare us", or other similar phrases that acknowledge God as Lord. When one or more saints are addressed, the response, usually a simple "pray for us" reflects our need for the help of the saints in heaven. If saints are included, our Blessed Lady is addressed first. The litany ends with a threefold prayer to the Lamb of God who takes away the sins of the world, followed by a final prayer which first acknowledges God's works and blessings received, then implores God to hear our prayers and help us live according to his will.

Praying with litanies

Litanies combine several elements of prayer, making them suitable for all ages and for many occasions.

They are prayers of blessing and adoration, making them encounters between God and mankind in a dialogue of love which is the primary meaning of prayer.

They are prayers of petition – our most usual form of prayer in this vale of tears as we turn back to the Father. We ask forgiveness, we search for the coming of God's Kingdom and we pray for every conceivable need.

They are prayers of intercession for others, "… characteristic of a heart attuned to God's mercy" as when Abraham begged God for mercy on the inhabitants of Sodom and Gomorrah (*Gen* 18).

And litanies are prayers of thanksgiving, rooted and grounded in the Eucharist which is the thanksgiving prayer of the Church.

Litanies are also prayers of joyful praise by which the Spirit is joined to our spirits to bear witness that we are children of God. Litanies of praise help to carry forward all the other forms of prayer towards God our Father, the source of our life.[4]

Christian prayer

Litanies combine in themselves the three forms of expression taken by Christian prayer.

• They are vocal prayers, spoken in communion with others, but expressed from the believer's own heart. Our Lord understood the human need to involve the senses in prayer when he taught his disciples the Our Father. We are unique creatures with bodies such as animals have, but with spirits also, as the angels are. We need interior prayer for our spirits, but we also need to involve our bodies in vocal prayer.

• They are opportunities for encouraging meditative prayer as the images evoked engage with our own thoughts, imagination, emotion, and desire and help us pass from thought to reality.

• Litanies can also help prepare the heart for contemplative prayer in which we consent to abide and keep watch with the Lord for a while, even though our senses are calling for sleep, food or entertainment.[5]

Praying litanies

Everyone can fruitfully engage in the praying of litanies. Children love the repetition of the words which they know, they are happy to participate by leading a section; they are attracted by beautiful symbolism and they are usually comfortable with the length and predictable limits of the prayer (a litany can of course be shortened for private use and adapted to the needs of children).

Used at a prayer group, a litany gives everyone a means by which to participate without discomfort and can encourage individual vocal prayer to follow. A litany said after Mass has ended can provide a reflective bridge between the Holy Sacrifice and the return to daily life. Elderly people and the partially sighted or deaf are able to participate in this form of prayer which can support their failing senses and give them a sense of inclusion. Litanies prayed in the home are a practical way for families to begin to engage in prayer together; prayed with the sick and dying they can comfort by their gentle rhythm and movement. Used in processions – their original use – they promote the cohesion and mutual support of the community.

Litanies of the Church Officially Approved for Public Use

The six approved Litanies

Clement VIII allowed only two litanies of the eighty or more which were in circulation in 1601:

- The Litany of Saints – the oldest of the litanies

- The Litany of Loreto to Our Lady

Since the time of Clement VIII, four more litanies have been added to the list of litanies approved for public worship.

- The Litany of the Holy Name of Jesus

- The Litany of the Sacred Heart of Jesus

- The Litany of St Joseph

- The Litany of the Most Precious Blood

These six litanies each carry a partial indulgence.[6]

Litany of the Saints

Pope Gregory the Great seems to have formalised this litany which was already popular, declaring that it be sung for three days at the start of Lent as well as other times. The Litany of the Saints was also used in a thanksgiving procession he ordered for the end of a great plague in 590.

This litany is used in our own Liturgy. We find it incorporated (in an abridged form) into the Easter Vigil on Holy Saturday, into Ordination Masses, and used on Rogation Days (now optional, so not often observed) and around the time of All Saints and All Souls. It is used also for special occasions, such as the consecration of a church and at the funeral of a Pope. Many people will remember the moving and beautiful singing of this litany at the transferral of the body of St John Paul II to the Basilica of St Peter in 2005.

The saints included in this litany predate the canonisation process we know today; saints were declared as such by popular acclamation and by martyrdom. The number of saints included has grown over the years, and often saints are added for particular occasions and needs.

The Litany

In the name of the Father and of the Son and of the Holy Spirit. Amen.

Lord, have mercy
Lord, have mercy
Christ, have mercy
Christ, have mercy
Lord, have mercy
Lord, have mercy

Holy Mary, Mother of God,
pray for us
Holy Virgin of virgins,
pray for us
St Michael,
pray for us
Holy angels of God
pray for us
Abraham, our father in faith
pray for us
David, leader of
God's people
pray for us
All holy patriarchs
and prophets
pray for us

St John the Baptist
pray for us
St Joseph
pray for us
St Peter and St Paul
pray for us
St Andrew
pray for us
St John
pray for us
St Mary Magdalen
pray for us
St Stephen
pray for us
St Ignatius of Antioch
pray for us
St Lawrence
pray for us
St Perpetua and
St Felicity
pray for us
St Agnes
pray for us

St Gregory
pray for us
St Augustine
pray for us
St Athanasius
pray for us
St Basil
pray for us
St Martin
pray for us
St Benedict
pray for us
St Francis and St Dominic
pray for us
St Francis Xavier
pray for us
St John Vianney
pray for us
St Catherine of Siena
pray for us
St Teresa of Jesus
pray for us

Other saints may be included here

All holy men and women,
saints of God
pray for us

Lord, be merciful
Lord, deliver us we pray
From all evil
Lord, save your people
From every sin
Lord, save your people
From Satan's power
Lord, save your people
At the moment of death
Lord, save your people
From everlasting death
Lord, save your people
On the day of judgement
Lord, save your people

By your Incarnation
Lord, save your people
By your suffering and cross
Lord, save your people
By your Death and
Resurrection
Lord, save your people
By your return in glory
to the Father
Lord, save your people
By the outpouring of the
Holy Spirit
Lord, save your people

By your coming again
in glory
Lord, save your people

Be merciful to us sinners
Lord, we ask you,
hear our prayer
Guide and protect your
holy Church
Lord, we ask you,
hear our prayer

Keep the pope and all the
clergy in faithful service
to your Church
Lord, we ask you,
hear our prayer

Bring all peoples together
in love and peace
Lord, we ask you,
hear our prayer

Strengthen us in your
service
Lord, we ask you,
hear our prayer

Jesus, Son of the Living God
Lord, we ask you,
hear our prayer

Christ, hear us
Christ, hear us
Christ, graciously hear us
Christ, graciously hear us

Let us pray.
God of our ancestors who set their hearts on you, of those
who fell asleep in peace, and of those who won the martyrs'
violent crown: we are surrounded by these witnesses as by
clouds of fragrant incense. In this age we would be counted
in this communion of all the saints; keep us always in their
good and blessed company. In their midst we make every
prayer through Christ who is our Lord for ever and ever.
Amen.

Litany of Loreto to Our Lady

This is the only other litany permitted by Clement VIII; it had already been approved and promoted by Pope Sixtus V in 1587. There is not a great deal known about its origins before his time, but clearly some form of it was in existence and in regular use by then. Earlier Marian litanies tended to be very long and were probably intended more for individual use, but gradually they were shortened and brought into public use, especially at times of epidemics or other great need in the way that the Litany of the Saints was used. The Litany of Loreto seems to have developed along the same lines as other Marian litanies of the time, but its popularity and survival probably stem from its use at the Holy House of Loreto, from where pilgrims from all over Christendom brought it back to their own countries and parishes.

This litany is perhaps the most poetic and beautiful, consisting of a series of petitions which express the wonderful gift of grace given to Mary and completed in her in a way we cannot yet achieve. A shortened form of this litany can be particularly helpful in use with children who are often drawn to the symbolic images such as "tower of ivory", "morning star", "queen of angels" and "mystical rose".

The Litany

In the name of the Father and of the Son and of the Holy Spirit. Amen.

Lord, have mercy
Lord, have mercy
Christ, have mercy
Christ have mercy
Lord, have mercy
Lord, have mercy

God our Father in heaven
have mercy on us
God the Son, Redeemer of the world
have mercy on us
God the Holy Spirit
have mercy on us
Holy Trinity, one God
have mercy on us

Holy Mary
pray for us
Holy Mother of God
pray for us
Holy Virgin of virgins
pray for us

Mother of Christ,
pray for us
Mother of the Church
pray for us
Mother of divine grace
pray for us
Mother most pure
pray for us
Mother most chaste
pray for us
Mother inviolate
pray for us
Mother undefiled
pray for us
Mother most amiable
pray for us
Mother most admirable
pray for us
Mother of good counsel
pray for us
Mother of our Creator
pray for us

Mother of our Saviour
pray for us
Virgin most prudent
pray for us
Virgin most venerable
pray for us
Virgin most renowned
pray for us
Virgin most powerful
pray for us
Virgin most merciful
pray for us
Virgin most faithful
pray for us
Mirror of justice
pray for us
Seat of wisdom
pray for us
Cause of our joy
pray for us
Spiritual vessel,
pray for us
Vessel of honour
pray for us
Singular vessel of devotion
pray for us

Mystical rose
pray for us
Tower of David
pray for us
Tower of ivory
pray for us
House of gold
pray for us
Ark of the covenant
pray for us
Gate of heaven
pray for us
Morning star
pray for us
Health of the sick
pray for us
Refuge of sinners
pray for us
Comforter of the afflicted
pray for us
Help of Christians
pray for us
Queen of angels
pray for us
Queen of patriarchs
pray for us

Queen of prophets
pray for us
Queen of apostles
pray for us
Queen of martyrs
pray for us
Queen of confessors
pray for us
Queen of virgins
pray for us
Queen of all saints
pray for us
Queen conceived without
original sin
pray for us
Queen assumed into heaven
pray for us
Queen of the most holy
Rosary
pray for us

Queen of the family
pray for us
Queen of peace
pray for us

Lamb of God, you take
away the sins of the world
spare us, O Lord
Lamb of God, you take
away the sins of the world
graciously hear us, O Lord
Lamb of God, you take
away the sins of the world
have mercy on us

Pray for us, O holy Mother
of God
*that we may be made worthy
of the promises of Christ*

Let us pray.
Eternal God, let your people enjoy constant health in mind
and body. Through the intercession of the Virgin Mary free
us from the sorrows of this life and lead us to happiness in
the life to come. Grant this through Christ our Lord. Amen.

Litany of the
Holy Name of Jesus

This is another old and beautiful litany making use of poetic language and symbolism. It was known as far back as the time of Pope Sixtus V (1585-90). Approved in an earlier form by Pius IX in 1862, it was then permitted for the whole world in 1886 by Leo XIII.

The Litany

In the name of the Father and of the Son and of the Holy Spirit. Amen.

Lord, have mercy
Lord, have mercy
Christ, have mercy
Christ, have mercy
Lord, have mercy
Lord, have mercy

God our Father in heaven
have mercy on us
God the Son, Redeemer
of the world
have mercy on us

God the Holy Spirit
have mercy on us
Holy Trinity, one God
have mercy on us

Jesus, Son of the
living God
have mercy on us
Jesus, splendour of
the Father
have mercy on us

Jesus, brightness of
everlasting light
have mercy on us
Jesus, king of glory
have mercy on us
Jesus, dawn of justice
have mercy on us
Jesus, Son of the Virgin
Mary
have mercy on us
Jesus, worthy of our love
have mercy on us
Jesus, worthy of our wonder
have mercy on us
Jesus, mighty God
have mercy on us
Jesus, father of the world
to come
have mercy on us
Jesus, prince of peace
have mercy on us
Jesus, all-powerful
have mercy on us
Jesus, pattern of patience
have mercy on us
Jesus, model of obedience
have mercy on us

Jesus, gentle and humble
of heart
have mercy on us
Jesus, lover of chastity
have mercy on us
Jesus, lover of us all
have mercy on us
Jesus, God of peace
have mercy on us
Jesus, author of life
have mercy on us
Jesus, model of goodness
have mercy on us
Jesus, seeker of souls
have mercy on us
Jesus, our God
have mercy on us
Jesus, our refuge
have mercy on us
Jesus, father of the poor
have mercy on us
Jesus, treasure of the faithful
have mercy on us
Jesus, Good Shepherd
have mercy on us
Jesus, the true light
have mercy on us

Jesus, eternal wisdom
have mercy on us
Jesus, infinite goodness
have mercy on us
Jesus, our way and our life
have mercy on us
Jesus, joy of angels
have mercy on us
Jesus, king of the patriarchs
have mercy on us
Jesus, teacher of apostles
have mercy on us
Jesus, master of evangelists
have mercy on us
Jesus, courage of martyrs
have mercy on us
Jesus, light of confessors
have mercy on us
Jesus, purity of virgins
have mercy on us
Jesus, crown of all saints
have mercy on us

Lord, be merciful
Jesus, save your people
From all evil
Jesus, save your people

From every sin
Jesus, save your people
From the snares
of the devil
Jesus, save your people
From your anger
Jesus, save your people
From the spirit
of infidelity
Jesus, save your people
From everlasting death
Jesus, save your people
From neglect of your
Holy Spirit
Jesus, save your people
By the mystery of your
Incarnation
Jesus, save your people
By your birth
Jesus, save your people
By your childhood
Jesus, save your people
By your hidden life
Jesus, save your people
By your public ministry
Jesus, save your people

By your agony and
crucifixion
Jesus, save your people
By your abandonment
Jesus, save your people
By your grief and sorrow
Jesus, save your people
By your death and burial
Jesus, save your people
By your rising to new life
Jesus, save your people
By your return in glory to
the Father
Jesus, save your people
By your gift of the Holy
Eucharist
Jesus, save your people

By your joy and glory
Jesus, save your people
Christ, hear us
Christ, hear us
Lord Jesus, hear our prayer
Lord Jesus, hear our prayer

Lamb of God, you take
away the sins of the world
have mercy on us
Lamb of God, you take
away the sins of the world
have mercy on us
Lamb of God, you take
away the sins of the world
have mercy on us

Let us pray.
Lord, may we who honour the holy name of Jesus enjoy
his friendship in this life and be filled with eternal joy in
the Kingdom where he lives and reigns for ever and ever.
Amen.

Litany of the Sacred Heart of Jesus

This litany was authorised in 1899, also by Leo XIII and is often used on the First Fridays of the month as a way of expressing sorrow for sins committed against the Sacred Heart of Jesus which is so full of love for us. St Margaret Mary had made the devotion to the Sacred Heart well known through the visions she received in 1673-1675 and several litanies developed during the following years. The litany as we now have it is an amalgamation of these, consisting of thirty-three petitions – one for each year of our Lord's life.

The Litany

In the name of the Father and of the Son and of the Holy Spirit. Amen.

Lord, have mercy
Lord, have mercy
Christ, have mercy
Christ, have mercy
Lord, have mercy
Lord, have mercy

God our Father of Heaven
have mercy on us
God the Son, Redeemer
of the world
have mercy on us
God, the Holy Spirit
have mercy on us

Holy Trinity, One God
have mercy on us
Heart of Jesus, Son of the
Eternal Father
have mercy on us
Heart of Jesus, formed by
the Holy Spirit in the womb
of the Virgin Mother
have mercy on us
Heart of Jesus, one with
the eternal Word
have mercy on us
Heart of Jesus, infinite
in majesty
have mercy on us
Heart of Jesus, holy temple
of God
have mercy on us
Heart of Jesus, tabernacle
of the Most High
have mercy on us
Heart of Jesus, house of
God and gate of Heaven
have mercy on us
Heart of Jesus, aflame with
love for us
have mercy on us

Heart of Jesus, source of
justice and love
have mercy on us
Heart of Jesus, full of
goodness and love
have mercy on us
Heart of Jesus, wellspring
of all virtue
have mercy on us
Heart of Jesus, worthy of
all praise
have mercy on us
Heart of Jesus, king and
centre of all hearts
have mercy on us
Heart of Jesus, treasure-
house of wisdom and
knowledge
have mercy on us
Heart of Jesus, in whom
there dwells the fullness
of God
have mercy on us
Heart of Jesus, in whom
the Father is well pleased
have mercy on us

Heart of Jesus, from whose
fullness we have all received
have mercy on us
Heart of Jesus, desire of
the eternal hills
have mercy on us
Heart of Jesus, patient
and full of mercy
have mercy on us
Heart of Jesus, generous
to all who turn to you
have mercy on us
Heart of Jesus, fountain
of life and holiness
have mercy on us
Heart of Jesus, atonement
for our sins
have mercy on us
Heart of Jesus,
overwhelmed with insults
have mercy on us
Heart of Jesus, broken for
our sins
have mercy on us
Heart of Jesus, obedient
even to death
have mercy on us

Heart of Jesus, pierced
by a lance
have mercy on us
Heart of Jesus, source of
all consolation
have mercy on us
Heart of Jesus, our life
and resurrection
have mercy on us
Heart of Jesus, our peace
and reconciliation
have mercy on us
Heart of Jesus, victim of
our sins
have mercy on us
Heart of Jesus, salvation
of all who trust in you
have mercy on us
Heart of Jesus, hope of
all who die in you
have mercy on us
Heart of Jesus, delight of
all the saints
have mercy on us

Lamb of God, you take
away the sins of the world
have mercy on us
Lamb of God, you take
away the sins of the world
have mercy on us

Lamb of God, you take
away the sins of the world
have mercy on us
Jesus, meek and humble
of heart
Touch our hearts and make
them like your own.

Let us pray.
Father, we rejoice in the gifts of love we have received from the heart of Jesus your Son. Open our hearts to share his life and continue to bless us with his love. We ask this in the name of Jesus the Lord. Amen.

Litany of St Joseph

This relatively recent litany was approved by Pope St Pius X on 18th March 1909. Devotion to St Joseph, whom Scripture describes as a "just man" (*Mt* 1:19), grew throughout the twentieth century and this litany is particularly suitable for families to pray together, placing themselves under his protection. The relatively short length of this litany may also be an advantage here.

The Litany

In the name of the Father and of the Son and of the Holy Spirit. Amen.

Lord, have mercy
Lord, have mercy
Christ, have mercy
Christ, have mercy
Lord, have mercy
Lord, have mercy

God our Father in heaven
have mercy on us
God the Son, Redeemer of the world
have mercy on us

God the Holy Spirit
have mercy on us
Holy Trinity, one God
have mercy on us
Holy Mary
pray for us
St Joseph
pray for us
Noble son of the House of David
pray for us

Light of patriarchs
pray for us
Husband of the Mother
of God
pray for us
Guardian of the Virgin
pray for us
Foster father of the Son
of God
pray for us
Faithful guardian of Christ
pray for us
Head of the Holy Family
pray for us
Joseph, chaste and just
pray for us
Joseph, prudent and brave
pray for us
Joseph, obedient and loyal
pray for us
Pattern of patience
pray for us
Lover of poverty
pray for us
Model of workers
pray for us
Example to parents
pray for us

Guardian of virgins
pray for us
Pillar of family life
pray for us
Comfort of the troubled
pray for us
Hope of the sick
pray for us
Patron of the dying
pray for us
Terror of evil spirits
pray for us
Protector of the Church
pray for us

Lamb of God, you take
away the sins of the world
have mercy on us
Lamb of God, you take
away the sins of the world
have mercy on us
Lamb of God, you take
away the sins of the world
have mercy on us
God made him master
of his household
*and put him in charge of
all that he owned*

Let us pray.
Almighty God, in your infinite wisdom and love you chose Joseph to be the husband of Mary, the mother of your Son. As we enjoy his protection on earth may we have the help of his prayers in heaven. We ask this through Christ our Lord. Amen.

Litany of the Most Precious Blood

This, the most recent addition to the list of litanies for public recitation, was promulgated by Pope St John XXIII on 24th February 1960.[7] The feast of the Precious Blood itself was established in 1849 by Pius IX. Although this litany is relatively recent, devotion to the Precious Blood of Jesus dates back to the earliest days of Christianity when it was recognised that the Church herself and her sacraments were born from the wounded side of Our Lord.

The Litany

In the name of the Father and of the Son and of the Holy Spirit. Amen.

Lord, have mercy
Lord, have mercy
Christ, have mercy
Christ, have mercy
Lord, have mercy
Lord, have mercy

God our Father in heaven
have mercy on us

God the Son, Redeemer of the world
have mercy on us
God the Holy Spirit
have mercy on us
Holy Trinity, one God
have mercy on us

Blood of Christ, only Son
of the Father
save us

Blood of Christ, Incarnate
Word
save us

Blood of Christ, of the new
and eternal covenant
save us

Blood of Christ, that spilled
to the ground
save us

Blood of Christ, shed
profusely at the scourging
save us

Blood of Christ, dripping
from the thorns
save us

Blood of Christ, shed on
the Cross
save us

Blood of Christ, the price
of our redemption
save us

Blood of Christ, our only
claim to pardon
save us

Blood of Christ, our
blessing cup
save us

Blood of Christ, in which
we are washed
save us

Blood of Christ, torrent
of mercy
save us

Blood of Christ, that
overcomes evil
save us

Blood of Christ, strength
of the martyrs
save us

Blood of Christ, endurance
of the saints
save us

Blood of Christ, that makes
the barren fruitful
save us

Blood of Christ, protection
of the threatened
save us

Blood of Christ, comfort
of the weary
save us

Blood of Christ, solace of
the mourner
save us
Blood of Christ, hope of
the repentant
save us
Blood of Christ,
consolation of the dying
save us
Blood of Christ, our peace
and refreshment
save us
Blood of Christ, our pledge
of life
save us
Blood of Christ, by which
we pass to glory
save us

Blood of Christ, most
worthy of honour
save us

Lamb of God, you take
away the sins of the world
have mercy on us
Lamb of God, you take
away the sins of the world
have mercy on us
Lamb of God, you take
away the sins of the world
have mercy on us

Lord, you redeemed us by
your Blood
you have made us
a Kingdom to serve
our God

Let us pray.
Father, by the Blood of your Son you have set us free and
saved us from death. Continue your work of love within us,
that by constantly celebrating the mystery of our salvation
we may reach the eternal life it promises. We ask this
through Christ our Lord. Amen.

LITANIES FOR PRIVATE USE

In addition to the six litanies approved for public use, there are many other litanies in circulation. Not all of these express ideas which are in full accordance with the teachings of the Church, so caution must be exercised in the choice of litanies to be prayed privately. The litanies which follow are suggestions which may be helpful:

• Litany of the Forty Martyrs of England and Wales

• Litany of the Passion

• Litany of the Resurrection

• Litany of Our Lord Jesus Christ, Priest and Victim

• Litany to St John Paul II

• Litany to the Divine Mercy

• Litany of Humility.

Litany of the Forty Martyrs of England and Wales

On 25th October 1970, Pope Paul VI canonized the Forty Martyrs of England and Wales, "to the glory of the holy and undivided Trinity, for the honour of the universal faith and the advancement of Christian life". The forty were chosen from among the hundreds of those who, in the dark days of the persecution of faithful Catholics, had died for the faith.[8]

The Litany

In the name of the Father and of the Son and of the Holy Spirit. Amen.

Lord, have mercy
Lord, have mercy
Christ, have mercy
Christ, have mercy
Lord, have mercy
Lord, have mercy

God our Father in heaven
have mercy on us

God the Son, Redeemer
of the world
have mercy on us
God the Holy Spirit,
have mercy on us
Holy Trinity, one God
have mercy on us

Mary, Queen of apostles
pray for us
Mary, Queen of martyrs
pray for us

St John Houghton
pray for us
St Richard Reynolds
pray for us
St Augustine Webster
pray for us
St Robert Lawrence
pray for us
St John Stone
pray for us
St Cuthbert Mayne
pray for us
St Edmund Campion
pray for us
St Ralph Sherwin
pray for us
St Alexander Briant
pray for us
St John Paine
pray for us
St Luke Kirby
pray for us

St Richard Gwyn
pray for us
St Margaret Clitherow
pray for us
St Margaret Ward
pray for us
St Edmund Gennings
pray for us
St Swithun Wells
pray for us
St Polydore Plasden
pray for us
St Eustace White
pray for us
St John Boste
pray for us
St Robert Southwell
pray for us
St Henry Walpole
pray for us
St Philip Howard
pray for us
St John Jones
pray for us
St John Rigby
pray for us

St Anne Line
pray for us
St Nicholas Owen
pray for us
St Thomas Garnet
pray for us
St John Roberts
pray for us
St John Almond
pray for us
St Edmund Arrowsmith
pray for us
St Ambrose Barlow
pray for us
St Alban Roe
pray for us

St Henry Morse
pray for us
St John Southworth
pray for us
St John Plessington
pray for us
St Philip Evans
pray for us
St John Lloyd
pray for us
St John Wall
pray for us
St John Kemble
pray for us
St David Lewis
pray for us

Let us pray.

O God, in whom there is no change or shadow of alteration, you gave courage to the holy martyrs. Grant us, we beseech you, through their intercession, the grace to always value the Holy Mass. May we be strengthened to serve you in imitation of the courage of these holy martyrs. We ask this through Jesus Christ, your Son, who lives and reigns with you in the unity of the Holy Spirit, one God, for ever and ever. Amen.

Litany of the Passion

(Bl. John Henry Newman)

Blessed John Henry Newman was, as is well known, a convert to Catholicism (1845), and we see in this litany how he meditated upon the sufferings of our Lord. This is part of a whole scheme of litanies written by Newman for use at various times of the year;[9] this one is suggested for the latter part of Lent.

The Litany

In the name of the Father and of the Son and of the Holy Spirit. Amen.

Lord, have mercy
Lord, have mercy
Christ, have mercy
Christ, have mercy
Lord, have mercy
Lord, have mercy
Christ, hear us
Christ, graciously hear us

God the Father of Heaven
have mercy on us
God the Son, Redeemer of the world
have mercy on us
God the Holy Ghost
have mercy on us
Holy Trinity, one God
have mercy on us

Jesus, the Eternal Wisdom
have mercy on us
The Word made flesh
have mercy on us
Hated by the world
have mercy on us
Sold for thirty pieces
of silver
have mercy on us
Sweating blood in your
agony
have mercy on us
Betrayed by Judas
have mercy on us
Forsaken by your disciples
have mercy on us
Struck upon the cheek
have mercy on us
Accused by false witnesses
have mercy on us
Spit upon in the face
have mercy on us
Denied by Peter
have mercy on us
Mocked by Herod
have mercy on us

Scourged by Pilate
have mercy on us
Rejected for Barabbas
have mercy on us
Loaded with the cross
have mercy on us
Crowned with thorns
have mercy on us
Stripped of your garments
have mercy on us
Nailed to the tree
have mercy on us
Reviled by passers-by
have mercy on us
Scoffed at by the
malefactor
have mercy on us
Wounded in the side
have mercy on us
Shedding your last drop
of blood
have mercy on us
Forsaken by your Father
have mercy on us
Dying for our sins
have mercy on us

Taken down from the cross
have mercy on us
Laid in the sepulchre
have mercy on us
Rising gloriously
have mercy on us
Ascending into heaven
have mercy on us
Sending down the Paraclete
have mercy on us
Jesus our sacrifice
have mercy on us
Jesus our mediator
have mercy on us
Jesus our judge
have mercy on us

Be merciful
spare us, O Lord
Be merciful
graciously hear us, O Lord

From all sin
Lord Jesus, deliver us
From all evil
Lord Jesus, deliver us
From anger and hatred
Lord Jesus, deliver us

From malice and revenge
Lord Jesus, deliver us
From unbelief and
hardness of heart
Lord Jesus, deliver us
From blasphemy and
sacrilege
Lord Jesus, deliver us
From hypocrisy and
covetousness
Lord Jesus, deliver us
From blindness of the
understanding
Lord Jesus, deliver us
From contempt of your
warnings
Lord Jesus, deliver us
From relapse after your
judgements
Lord Jesus, deliver us
From danger of soul
and body
Lord Jesus, deliver us
From everlasting death
Lord Jesus, deliver us

We sinners
we beseech you, hear us

That you would spare us
we beseech you, hear us
That you would pardon us
we beseech you, hear us
That you would defend
your Church
we beseech you, hear us
That you would bless
your own
we beseech you, hear us
That you would convert
your foes
we beseech you, hear us
That you would spread
the truth
we beseech you, hear us
That you would destroy
error
we beseech you, hear us
That you would break
to pieces false gods
we beseech you, hear us
That you would increase
your elect

we beseech you, hear us
That you would let loose
the holy souls in prison
we beseech you, hear us
That you would unite us to
your Saints above
we beseech you, hear us

Lamb of God, you take
away the sins of the world
spare us, O Lord
Lamb of God, you take
away the sins of the world
graciously hear us, O Lord
Lamb of God, you take
away the sins of the world
have mercy on us
Christ, hear us
Christ, graciously hear us
Lord, have mercy
Christ, have mercy
Lord, have mercy

We adore you, O Christ,
and we bless you
*because through your
Holy Cross you did redeem
the world*

Let us pray.

O God, who for the redemption of the world was pleased to be born; to be circumcised; to be rejected; to be betrayed; to be bound with cords; to be led to the slaughter; to be shamefully gazed at; to be falsely accused; to be scourged and torn; to be spit upon, and crowned with thorns; to be mocked and reviled; to be buffeted and struck with rods; to be stripped; to be nailed to the cross; to be hoisted up thereon; to be reckoned among thieves; to have gall and vinegar to drink; to be pierced with a lance: through your most holy passion, which we, your sinful servants, call to mind, and by your holy cross and gracious death, deliver us from the pains of hell, and lead us where you led the thief who was crucified with you, who with the Father and the Holy Spirit lives and reigns, God, world without end. Amen.

Litany of the Resurrection

(Bl. John Henry Newman)

This litany is also part of Newman's scheme for the year; it is suggested for use from Easter Day until 1st May. The scheme does not seem to have been finished but the completed parts were published after Newman's death.[10]

The Litany

In the name of the Father and of the Son and of the Holy Spirit. Amen.

Lord, have mercy
Lord, have mercy
Christ, have mercy
Christ, have mercy
Lord, have mercy
Lord, have mercy

Christ, hear us
Christ, graciously hear us

God the Father of heaven
have mercy on us

God the Son, Redeemer of the world
have mercy on us
God the Holy Spirit
have mercy on us
Holy Trinity, one God
have mercy on us

Jesus, Redeemer of mankind
have mercy on us

Jesus, conqueror of sin
and Satan
have mercy on us
Jesus, triumphant over death
have mercy on us
Jesus, the Holy and the Just
have mercy on us
Jesus, the Resurrection
and the Life
have mercy on us
Jesus, the giver of grace
have mercy on us
Jesus, the Judge of the world
have mercy on us
Who laid down your life
for your sheep
have mercy on us
Who rose again the third day
have mercy on us
Who manifested yourself
to your chosen
have mercy on us
Visiting your blessed Mother
have mercy on us
Appearing to Mary
Magdalen while she wept
have mercy on us

Sending your angels to
the holy women
have mercy on us
Comforting the Eleven
have mercy on us
Saying to them, Peace
have mercy on us
Breathing on them the
Holy Spirit
have mercy on us
Confirming the faith
of Thomas
have mercy on us
Committing your flock
to Peter
have mercy on us
Speaking of the Kingdom
of God
have mercy on us

We sinners
we beseech you, hear us
That we may walk in
newness of life
we beseech you, hear us
That we may advance in
the knowledge of you
we beseech you, hear us

That we may grow in grace
we beseech you, hear us
That we may ever have
the bread of life
we beseech you, hear us
That we may persevere
unto the end
we beseech you, hear us
That we may have
confidence before you
at your coming
we beseech you, hear us
That we may behold your
face with joy
we beseech you, hear us
That we may be placed
at your right hand in the
judgement
we beseech you, hear us
That we may have our lot

with the saints
we beseech you, hear us

Lamb of God, you take
away the sins of the world
spare us, O Lord
Lamb of God, who takes
away the sins of the world
graciously hear us, O Lord
Lamb of God, who takes
away the sins of the world
have mercy on us

Christ, hear us
Christ, graciously hear us
Lord, have mercy
Christ, have mercy
Lord, have mercy
Christ is risen, alleluia
*he is risen indeed, and has
appeared to Simon, alleluia*

Let us pray.
O God, who by your only begotten Son have overcome death, and opened to us the way to eternal life, vouchsafe, we beseech you, so to confirm us by your grace, that we may in all things walk after the manner of those who have been redeemed from their sins, through the same Jesus Christ our Lord. Amen.

Litany of Our Lord Jesus Christ, Priest and Victim

This litany was apparently recited in the seminary at Kraków, especially on the eve of a priestly ordination and thus would have been prayed (in Latin) by Pope John Paul II as a seminarian there. He is said to have often prayed it in later life also.[11] The language is rich in symbolism and biblical imagery.[12]

The Litany

In the name of the Father and of the Son and of the Holy Spirit. Amen.

Lord, have mercy
Lord, have mercy
Christ, have mercy
Christ, have mercy
Lord, have mercy
Lord, have mercy
Christ hear us
Christ hear us
Christ, graciously hear us
Christ, graciously hear us

God our Father in heaven
have mercy on us
God the Son, Redeemer
of the world
have mercy on us
God the Holy Spirit
have mercy on us
Holy Trinity, one God
have mercy on us

Jesus, priest and victim
have mercy on us
Jesus, priest forever
according to the order of
Melchizedek
have mercy on us
Jesus, priest whom God
sent to preach the Gospel
to the poor
have mercy on us
Jesus, priest who at the Last
Supper instituted the form
of the eternal sacrifice
have mercy on us
Jesus, priest who lives
forever to intercede for us
have mercy on us
Jesus, High Priest whom
the Father anointed with
the Holy Spirit and power
have mercy on us
Jesus, High Priest chosen
from among men
have mercy on us
Jesus, made High Priest
for men
have mercy on us

Jesus, High Priest of our
confession of faith
have mercy on us
Jesus, High Priest of greater
glory than Moses
have mercy on us
Jesus, High Priest of the
true tabernacle
have mercy on us
Jesus, High Priest of the
good things to come
have mercy on us
Jesus, High Priest, holy,
innocent and undefiled
have mercy on us
Jesus, High Priest faithful
and merciful
have mercy on us
Jesus, High Priest inflamed
with zeal for God and souls,
have mercy on us
Jesus, High Priest, perfect
forever
have mercy on us
Jesus, High Priest, who by
your own blood entered
the heavens
have mercy on us

Jesus, High Priest, who
opened a new way for us
have mercy on us
Jesus, High Priest, who
loved us and washed us
from our sins in your blood
have mercy on us
Jesus, High Priest, who
offered yourself to God
as an oblation and
sacrificial victim
have mercy on us
Jesus, sacrificial victim of
God and men
have mercy on us
Jesus, holy and immaculate
sacrificial victim
have mercy on us
Jesus, pleasing sacrificial
victim
have mercy on us
Jesus, peace-making
sacrificial victim
have mercy on us
Jesus, sacrifice of
propitiation and praise
have mercy on us

Jesus, sacrificial victim of
reconciliation and peace
have mercy on us
Jesus, sacrificial victim in
whom we have confidence
and access to God
have mercy on us
Jesus, sacrificial victim
living forever and ever
have mercy on us

Be merciful
spare us, Jesus
Be merciful
graciously hear us, Jesus

From rashly entering
the clergy
deliver us, Jesus
From the sin of sacrilege
deliver us, Jesus
From the spirit of
incontinence
deliver us, Jesus
From sordid pursuits
deliver us, Jesus
From every lapse into
simony
deliver us, Jesus

From the unworthy
administration of the
Church's treasures
deliver us, Jesus
From the love of the world
and its vanities
deliver us, Jesus
From the unworthy
celebration of your
Mysteries
deliver us, Jesus
Through your eternal
priesthood
deliver us, Jesus
Through the holy anointing
whereby you were
constituted a priest by God
the Father
deliver us, Jesus
Through your priestly spirit
deliver us, Jesus
Through that ministry
whereby you glorified your
Father on earth
deliver us, Jesus
Through the bloody
immolation of yourself

made once and for all upon
the Cross
deliver us, Jesus
Through that same sacrifice
daily renewed upon the altar
deliver us, Jesus
Through that divine power
which you exercise invisibly
in your priests
deliver us, Jesus
That you would deign to
maintain the whole priestly
order in holy religion
we beseech you, hear us
That you would deign to
provide your people with
pastors after your own heart
we beseech you, hear us
That you would deign to fill
them with the spirit of your
priesthood
we beseech you, hear us
That the lips of your
priests might preserve true
knowledge
we beseech you, hear us
That you would deign to

send faithful workers into
your harvest
we beseech you, hear us
That you would deign
to multiply the faithful
dispensers of your Mysteries
we beseech you, hear us
That you would deign to
grant them perseverance in
the service of your will
we beseech you, hear us
That you would deign to
give them gentleness in their
ministry, resourcefulness in
their actions, and constancy
in prayer
we beseech you, hear us
That through them you
would deign to promote the
veneration of the Blessed

Sacrament everywhere
we beseech you, hear us
That you would deign to
receive into your joy those
who have served you well
we beseech you, hear us
Lamb of God, you take
away the sins of the world
spare us, O Lord
Lamb of God, you take
away the sins of the world
graciously hear us, O Lord
Lamb of God, you take
away the sins of the world
have mercy on us, O Lord
Jesus, our priest
hear us
Jesus, our priest
graciously hear us

Let us pray.
O God, sanctifier and guardian of your Church, raise up in
her through your Spirit suitable and faithful dispensers of
the holy mysteries, so that by their ministry and example,
the Christian people may be guided under your protection
in the path of salvation. Through Christ our Lord. Amen.

Litany to St John Paul II

St John Paul II was born in Poland in 1920, ordained priest in 1946 and bishop in 1958. He was elected pope in 1978, died in 2005 and was declared a saint on 27th April 2014. His feast day is 22nd October. The litany has an imprimatur, dated 12th April 2011, from Cardinal Stanisław Dziwisz, Archbishop of Kraków.[13]

The Litany

In the name of the Father and of the Son and of the Holy Spirit. Amen.

Kyrie eleison
Christe eleison
Kyrie eleison
Christ, hear us
Christ, graciously hear us

God our Father in Heaven
have mercy on us
God the Son, Redeemer of the world
have mercy on us
God, the Holy Spirit
have mercy on us

Holy Trinity, one God
have mercy on us

Holy Mary
pray for us
St John Paul II
pray for us
Immersed in the Father rich in mercy
pray for us
United with Christ, the Redeemer of man
pray for us

Filled with the Holy Spirit,
Lord and giver of life
pray for us
Completely devoted to Mary
pray for us
Friend of the saints and
blessed
pray for us
Successor of Peter and
the servant of servants
of God
pray for us
Guardian of the Church,
teaching the truths of faith
pray for us
Father of the Council and
executor of its intentions
pray for us
Supporting the unity of
Christians and the whole
human family
pray for us
Zealous lover of the
Eucharist
pray for us
Tireless pilgrim of the earth
pray for us

Missionary to all nations
pray for us
Witness of faith, hope,
and love
pray for us
Persistent sharer in the
sufferings of Christ
pray for us
Apostle of reconciliation
and peace
pray for us
Promoter of the civilization
of love
pray for us
Propagator of the new
evangelization
pray for us
Master calling us to sail
into the deep
pray for us
Teacher showing us
holiness as a measure
of life
pray for us
Pope of Divine Mercy
pray for us

High Priest gathering the
Church at the sacrifice
pray for us
Shepherd leading the flock
to heaven
pray for us
Brother and master of
priests
pray for us
Father of consecrated
persons
pray for us
Patron of Christian families
pray for us
Strengthener of spouses
pray for us
Defender of the unborn
pray for us
Protector of children
orphaned and abandoned
pray for us
Friend and teacher of the
young
pray for us
Good Samaritan for those
who suffer
pray for us

Supporter of the elderly
and lonely
pray for us
Propagator of the truth
about the dignity of man
pray for us
Man of prayer immersed
in God
pray for us
Lover of the liturgy
sacrificing at the altars
of the world
pray for us
The personification of
hard work
pray for us
Love in the cross of Christ
pray for us
Living your vocation
properly
pray for us
Patient in suffering
pray for us
Example of life and death
for the Lord
pray for us

Reprimanding sinners
pray for us
Showing the way to the
misguided
pray for us
Forgiving wrongdoers
pray for us
Respecting opponents and
persecutors
pray for us
Spokesman and defender of
the persecuted
pray for us
Supporter of the
unemployed
pray for us
Friend of the homeless
pray for us
Visitor of prisoners
pray for us

Supporter of the weak
pray for us
Teacher of solidarity to
everybody
pray for us
Lamb of God, you take
away the sins of the world
spare us, Lord
Lamb of God, you take
away the sins of the world
hear us, Lord
Lamb of God who takes
away the sins of the world
have mercy on us
Pray for us, St John Paul
*So that we would proclaim
to the world, with life and
words, Christ the Redeemer
of man*

Let us pray.

Merciful God, accept our thanksgiving for the gift of St John Paul's II apostolic life and mission. Through his intercession, help us grow in love for you and proclaim boldly the love of Christ to all people. Through Christ our Lord. Amen.

Litany to the Divine Mercy

St John Paul II wished to remind the world of the boundless mercy of God, and in the year 2000 he pronounced that the first Sunday after Easter (Low Sunday, the Second Sunday of Easter) would be known throughout the Church as Divine Mercy Sunday. In this Litany we ask for the mercy of God for ourselves and for others, we express our trust in his mercy and ask for God's help in showing his mercy to others.

The Litany

In the name of the Father and of the Son and of the Holy Spirit. Amen.

Lord, have mercy
Lord, have mercy
Christ, have mercy
Christ, have mercy
Lord, have mercy
Lord, have mercy

Christ, hear us
Christ, graciously hear us

God our Father in heaven
have mercy on us
God the Son, Redeemer of the world,
have mercy on us
God the Holy Spirit
have mercy on us
Holy Trinity, one God
have mercy on us

Divine Mercy, greatest attribute of God
we trust in you
Divine Mercy, unfathomable love of the Sanctifier
we trust in you
Divine Mercy, incomprehensible mystery of the Most Blessed Trinity
we trust in you
Divine Mercy, expression of the greatest might of God
we trust in you
Divine Mercy, in creation of heavenly spirits
we trust in you
Divine Mercy, in calling us forth from nothingness to existence
we trust in you
Divine Mercy, encompassing the whole universe
we trust in you
Divine Mercy, endowing us with immortal life
we trust in you
Divine Mercy, shielding us from deserved punishment
we trust in you
Divine Mercy, lifting us from the misery of sin
we trust in you
Divine Mercy, justifying us through the Person of the Incarnate Word
we trust in you
Divine Mercy, which flowed out from the wounds of Christ
we trust in you
Divine Mercy, gushing forth from the Sacred Heart of Jesus
we trust in you
Divine Mercy, giving us the Blessed Virgin Mary as Mother of Mercy
we trust in you
Divine Mercy, in revealing the mysteries of God
we trust in you
Divine Mercy, in the founding of Holy Church
we trust in you

Divine Mercy, in instituting the Holy Sacraments
we trust in you

Divine Mercy, first of all in the sacraments of Baptism and Penance
we trust in you

Divine Mercy, in the Holy Eucharist and the sacrament of Holy Orders
we trust in you

Divine Mercy, in calling us to the holy faith
we trust in you

Divine Mercy, in the conversion of sinners
we trust in you

Divine Mercy, in sanctifying the just
we trust in you

Divine Mercy, in perfecting the pious
we trust in you

Divine Mercy, fount of help for the sick and the suffering
we trust in you

Divine Mercy, relief for anguished hearts
we trust in you

Divine Mercy, only hope of despairing souls
we trust in you

Divine Mercy, accompanying us in every moment of our lives
we trust in you

Divine Mercy, anticipating our needs with graces
we trust in you

Divine Mercy, repose of the dying
we trust in you

Divine Mercy, heavenly delight of the saved
we trust in you

Divine Mercy, respite and relief of the souls in Purgatory
we trust in you

Divine Mercy, crown of All Saints
we trust in you

Divine Mercy, inexhaustible
source of miracles
we trust in you
Lamb of God, who revealed
the greatest mercy in
redeeming the world by
dying on the cross
spare us, O Lord
Lamb of God, who
mercifully offer yourself for
our sake in every holy Mass
graciously hear us, O Lord
Lamb of God, who
takes away our sins with
inexhaustible compassion
have mercy on us
The mercy of God is above
all his works
hence we will praise
the Divine Mercy for ever
and ever

Let us pray.

Eternal God, in whom mercy is endless and whose treasury of compassion inexhaustible, look kindly upon us and increase your mercy in us, that in difficult moments we might not despair nor become despondent, but with great confidence submit ourselves to your holy will, which is love and mercy itself. Through our Lord Jesus Christ, king of mercy, who with you and the Holy Spirit shows us mercy now and for ever. Amen.

Litany of Humility

This is usually attributed to Servant of God Rafael Cardinal Merry del Val (1865-1930), Secretary of State under Pope St Pius X, although (perhaps aptly enough) some have claimed it wasn't in fact written by him but by someone else inspired by his writings. In its original form, this litany does not have the usual beginning and ending; these have been attached for the sake of consistency and convenience, but can of course be omitted.

The Litany

In the name of the Father and of the Son and of the Holy Spirit. Amen.

Lord, have mercy
Lord, have mercy
Christ, have mercy
Christ, have mercy
Lord, have mercy
Lord, have mercy
Christ, hear us.
Christ, graciously hear us.

God our Father in heaven
have mercy on us
God the Son, Redeemer of the world
have mercy on us
God the Holy Spirit
have mercy on us
Holy Trinity, one God
have mercy on us

Holy Mary, Mother of God
pray for us

O Jesus! meek and humble
of heart
hear me
From the desire of being
esteemed
deliver me, Jesus
From the desire of being
loved
deliver me, Jesus
From the desire of being
extolled
deliver me, Jesus
From the desire of being
honoured
deliver me, Jesus
From the desire of being
praised
deliver me, Jesus
From the desire of being
preferred to others
deliver me, Jesus
From the desire of being
consulted
deliver me, Jesus

From the desire of being
approved
deliver me, Jesus
From the fear of being
humiliated
deliver me, Jesus
From the fear of being
despised
deliver me, Jesus
From the fear of suffering
rebukes
deliver me, Jesus
From the fear of being
calumniated
deliver me, Jesus
From the fear of being
forgotten
deliver me, Jesus
From the fear of being
ridiculed
deliver me, Jesus
From the fear of being
wronged
deliver me, Jesus
From the fear of being
suspected
deliver me, Jesus

That others may be loved
more than I
*Jesus, grant me the grace to
desire it*
That others may be
esteemed more than I
*Jesus, grant me the grace to
desire it*
That, in the opinion of the
world, others may increase
and I may decrease
*Jesus, grant me the grace to
desire it*
That others may be chosen
and I set aside
*Jesus, grant me the grace to
desire it*

That others may be praised
and I unnoticed
*Jesus, grant me the grace to
desire it*
That others may be
preferred to me in
everything
*Jesus, grant me the grace to
desire it*
That others may become
holier than I, provided that
I may become as holy as
I should
*Jesus, grant me the grace to
desire it*

Let us pray.
O God, whose only Son lived humbly among us and died
in great humility to save us, grant that we may always strive
to follow his example in desiring humility for the sake of
the Gospel. Through Christ our Lord. Amen.

Praying with Litanies
Through the Year

Through the praying of these litanies, the faith of Christians can be strengthened, thoughts focused and community bonds reinforced. Of course, any of them may be prayed at any time, bearing in mind that only six are authorised for public use, but it may be helpful to offer some suggestions as to the different months of the year when these litanies might be especially appropriate.

JANUARY has long been regarded as the month of the Holy Name of Jesus; the New Year is a good time to remember to love and bless his name in the Litany of the Holy Name of Jesus.

FEBRUARY is when Lent often begins, or is drawing near - an appropriate month to meditate using the Litany of Our Lord Jesus Christ, Priest and Victim.

MARCH is often the month of Lent and the Triduum; the Litany of the Passion or the Litany of Humility would fit well here. The Litany of St Joseph could be prayed in March for his Feast on the 19th.

APRIL is usually the month of Easter, so the Litany of the Resurrection would be most suitable. The Divine Mercy Litany could be prayed in April, which would be the most likely month for that feast.

MAY, although dedicated to our Blessed Lady, also begins with the feast of St Joseph the Worker, making it a good month to use the Litany of St Joseph. The Litany of Loreto to Our Lady could equally well be chosen for Mary's month of May.

JUNE is traditionally the month dedicated to the Sacred Heart of Jesus, and the Solemnity of the Sacred Heart almost always occurs in this month, so the Litany of the Sacred Heart of Jesus fits well here.

JULY has traditionally been dedicated to the precious blood of Jesus. The Litany of the Most Precious Blood is therefore a good choice for this month.

AUGUST is known as the month of devotion to the Holy Eucharist and also of the Immaculate Heart of Mary. Given the devotion St John Paul II had for both these, August could be an appropriate month for the Litany to St John Paul II.

SEPTEMBER is the month for remembering the sorrows of Our Lady; the martyrdoms of the 16th and 17th century must have grieved her terribly in addition to all the sorrows she felt for her Son. During this month we could pray the Litany of the Forty Martyrs of England and Wales.

OCTOBER is well known as the month of the Rosary and we recall Our Lady's help in the Battle of Lepanto in October 1571. The Litany of Loreto to Our Lady would be a good choice here.

NOVEMBER begins with the great feast of All Saints, but is thereafter dedicated to the Holy Souls in Purgatory. The Litany of the Saints could be offered for the Holy Souls during November.

DECEMBER brings us back to the start of the Church's year, and what better way to begin Advent than by remembering the mercy of God while praying the Litany to the Divine Mercy.

May all who use these litanies
be blessed in their prayer.

A Final Prayer

O God, who sent your only Son to become man, to suffer, die and rise again for our salvation; as he on earth taught us how to pray, so keep us faithful in prayer and good works that we may come at last with Blessed Mary and all the saints to your kingdom in heaven. Amen.

Endnotes

[1] All Scriptural quotations are taken from the Revised Standard Version of the Bible unless otherwise stated.

[2] *Daniel* 3; this version is taken from Morning Prayer of the Divine Office.

[3] *http://www.ocf.org/OrthodoxPage/liturgy/liturgy.html*

[4] Cf CCC 2626-2639.

[5] Cf CCC 2700-2719.

[6] *The Handbook of Indulgences*, par.29.

[7] These dates refer only to the time when the particular litany was approved for public use. Devotion to the worship of God from a particular aspect, e.g. the Sacred Heart, the Precious Blood, generally dates back much further.

[8] *https://www.catholicculture.org/culture/liturgicalyear/prayers/view.cfm?id=1311*

[9] *http://www.newmanreader.org/works/meditations/meditations7.html#litany1*

[10] Ian Ker, *The Catholic Revival in English Literature*, (Leominster, Gracewing, 2003), p.39.

[11] Ecclesiastical approval for English translation: - Adam Cardinal Maida, Archbishop of Detroit, rescript of 21st November 2008 ©2009 Congregazione dei Canonici Regolari della S. Croce, Roma *http://www.opusangelorum.org/Prayer/litanyforthepriest.html*

[12] Matthew Levering (ed.), *On the Priesthood: Classic and Contemporary Texts* (Oxford, Rowman & Littlefield, 2003), p.137.

[13] *http://sunday.niedziela.pl/artykul.php?dz=jpii&id_art=00077*

Novena to the Blessed Virgin Mary

Fr Walter Macken

This booklet is designed to reflect more deeply on Mary, Mother of God, during the days leading up to and around any of her feast days. Drawing from Scripture, Church teaching and recent papal teaching, Fr Macken offers valuable catechesis on Mary and her place in the life of the Christian's daily life. The Novena is centred around the themes of faith, simplicity, serenity, missionary spirit, practical humility, distractions, charity, confession and family life.

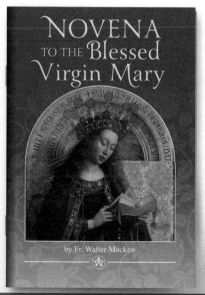

D765   ISBN 978 1 86082 882 9

Handbook of Novenas to the Saints

Glynn MacNiven-Johnston and Raymond Edwards

A novena is a way of praying, often for a particular intention or need. It consists, very simply, of a prayer or prayers said for nine (usually consecutive) days. This booklet contains newly composed novena prayers asking for the intercession of various saints. The long experience of praying Christians, and the teaching of the Church, assure us that the duty of Christians to support each other with prayer does not end with this life, and the saints delight to add their voices to ours when we make our requests to God our Father. Each novena is prefaced with a short biography of the saint.

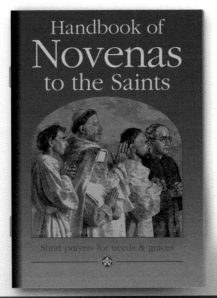

Handbook of
Novenas
to the Saints

Short prayers for needs & graces

D733   ISBN 978 1 86082 687 0

A Handbook of Scriptural Novenas
For Various Needs and Intentions

These newly composed novena prayers present figures from Scripture from whom we learn lessons in faith and prayer. The situations and difficulties they faced frequently mirror our own worries and concerns. Thus Hannah prays for the gift of children, Job learns to be honest with God, Martha complains that she does all the work, Deborah and Barak learn what to do when overwhelmed, and Jonah too when God's plan doesn't seem to make sense. These and other figures open the Scriptures to us, and we learn more of the Novenas as a form of prayer.

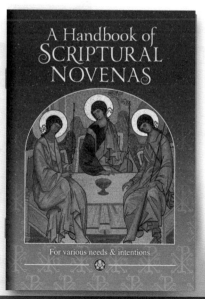

D798 ISBN: 978 1 78469 066 3